dream / arteries

Also by Phinder Dulai

*Basmati Brown: Paths, Passages, Cross and Open
Ragas from the Periphery*

PHINDER DULAI

dream / arteries

TALONBOOKS

Talonbooks
278 East First Avenue, Vancouver, British Columbia, Canada V5T 1A6
www.talonbooks.com

First printing: 2014

Typeset in Minion and Myriad
Printed and bound in Canada on 100% post-consumer recycled paper

Cover design by Typesmith
Cover photograph by Rennett Stowe, used under Flickr Creative Commons licence

Talonbooks gratefully acknowledges the financial support of the Canada Council for the Arts, the Government of Canada through the Canada Book Fund, and the Province of British Columbia through the British Columbia Arts Council and the Book Publishing Tax Credit.

Library and Archives Canada Cataloguing in Publication

Dulai, Phinder, author
        Dream/arteries / Phinder Dulai.

Poems.
Includes bibliographical references.
ISBN 978-0-88922-913-6 (pbk.)

        1. Komagatamaru (Ship)—Poetry. I. Title.

PS8557.U385D74 2014   C811'.54   C2014-903256-0

"A poet's work is to name the un-nameable, to point at frauds, to take sides, start arguments, shape the world, and stop it going to sleep."

– Salman Rushdie, *The Independent* (February 18, 1989) four days after a fatwa was pronounced against him in Iran because of *The Satanic Verses*

I ask the walking stones
about the heart-breaking incident

they laugh
turn their faces and walk away

– Sadhu Binning, "The Heart-Breaking Incident," *No More Watno Dur* (1994)

In memory of

Mewa Singh Lopoke

and for those who seek sanctuary

CONTENTS

an epistle to the reader (confidential)   xi

soul-journ to the end of the pacific   1

from fragments   41

    wisconsin temple poems   43
    mourning ghazals   46
    3 flag poems – dry skin draped over clay stones   52
    the rivers   55
    ants   56
    desert   58
    atomic eeyore   60
    smile   61
    chita – 100 lines to die   62
    rakhri   64

the world after tomorrow   65

    presence   67
    hollow   68
    waves   69
    dawn   70
    3:00 a.m.   71
    sleep walking   72
    pencil thought   73
    ash   74
    return   75
    swing   76
    asiancy (a word)   77
    of friends   79
    after tomorrow   80
    grief   82
    sadness   83
    it-dhé (here), a vancouver special circa 1980   84
    melancholy   85
    autumn drift   87

in conversation   89

> re-word   91
> slam   92
> the obesity in idea   94
> a man steps   97
> how lingua and i met in conversation   98
> in the room   100
> havana christmas – five interludes   101
> where love resides   107
>
> *acknowledgements*   109
> *source notes*   112
> *archival photos*   117
> *about the author*   120

Archival Note: The following is entered by
p. dulai as an introduction.

Public Record Notice: The above statement has
been proven to be incorrect and lacking in clear
facts (dated July 23, 2014 – dp)

KM File 10037 (Personal)

Book item opened and contents entered as record

P.S.D. / pd

                    Surrey, British Columbia, July 23, 2014

Dear R.E.A.D.E.R.,

Respected citizen of a country and inhabitor of the world,

Madam or Sir:

I beg to confirm the context of this letter.

The book accompanying this letter has been deposited into
your hands as an opportunity to uncover truths. Indeed, this
book sets out both a fictional and factual account of an
emigrant ship that had profound historical consequences —
impacting peoples' lives and future government laws on
immigration; thus the book examines what truth looks like in
the interstice between the public record and archival space.

This literary record is a response to the well-maintained factual records of the arrival of the Komagata Maru at Vancouver in the summer of 1914. So little is documented in the public record about the aspirations of passengers during the ordeal. Such a lack of interest shown by the surveillance procedures and reporting process for the passengers' ideas of what they were seeking in the New World and what they left behind certainly shows a profound administrative oversight if not a gap of empathy and good conscience.

As the authenticated author of this book, I beg to confirm with you now that you will find themes flow into one another and within and beside the other; and they do so in concentric ways. This structural idiosyncrasy is the result of numerous journeys, memories that drift into one another, and times that compress and expand. The inspirations are many and include my grandfather, who first arrived in the city of Mombasa, Kenya, in 1948 onboard a deep-sea dhow ship; he set up home in Nairobi, in 1952 he returned to India, and then a few years later returned to Kenya onboard the SS Kenya. In 1955, my grandmother arrived in Mombasa via the SS City of Bombay with five children, one of whom included my father. In 1961 he left Nairobi to return to the village to marry; then with his wife he boarded the SS Stratheden to journey on to Great Britain and finally reached a new life there. With the exception of the SS Stratheden, the ships that brought my extended family west were all built on the Clyde River in Glasgow, Scotland. It is the same place that another ship was built a half-century earlier, later arriving in Vancouver with passengers who sought new lives here. My sincere apologies for this obvious digression.

I leave with you the full description of the ship that was built to bring not just cargo, but also human capital. The ship's registry record included with this letter is verbatim.

And so begins a journey . . .

Your obedient servant,

Archival Interloper

Name: SS Stubbenhuk

Other Names: SS Sicilia (1894), SS Komagata Maru (1913), SS Heian Maru (1924)

Built: 1890

Launched: Wednesday, August 13, 1890

Vessel Type: Passenger cargo vessel

Vessel Description: Steel, screw steamer, 2 masts

Builder: Charles Connell & Company, Scotstoun, Glasgow (Yard No. 168)

Engine Builder: D. Rowan & Son, Glasgow

Propulsion: T3 cylinder (24, 39, 64 x 42in), 265 nominal horsepower, single screw, 11 knots

Tonnage: 2922 gross register tonnage

Length: 329 feet

Breadth: 41.5 feet

First Owner: Dampfschiffs Rhederdei "Hansa," Hamburg

Subsequent Owner and Registration History:

   1894 Hamburg-Amerika Line, Hamburg

   1913 Shinyei Kisen Goshi Kaisha, Dairen

   1917 Kawauchi Goshi Kaisha, Dairen

   1921 Yamashita Kisen K.K., Fusan

   1923 Kabafuto Kisen K.K., Nishinomiya

   1924 Kasahara Shoji K.K., Osaka

End Year: 1926

Status: Wrecked February 11, 1926

Maiden Voyage: October 19, 1890, departed Hamburg for Montreal, Quebec

Disposal Detail: 1926 wrecked near Cape Soyedomari, Hokkaido, on passage from Otaru to Muroran. Chartered by a group of Sikhs to sail to Vancouver.

dust barrels in the spotlight
spring runoff tipping our tongues
a scribe will not perish without this

then again
will our words survive us …

"What is done with a shipload of my people will determine whether we shall have peace in all parts of the empire."

– Gurdit Singh, May 1914

"What is done with a shipload of my
people will determine whether we shall
have peace in all parts of the empire."
— Gurdit Singh, May 1914

soul-journ to the end of the pacific

Dated May 10, 2014

To an unknown passenger (a letter to the *maru*):

When you arrive in the early hours of the morning, you will not see the grey-green sheath of the Georgia Strait; instead, you will look into the darkness and know you have entered a new land. You will see the dark waves as they push against the rusty ship.

The distance offers a few waking lights as they bleed across the dark waters and, in that moment, you will drift to slumber. The air, a sweet remnant of spring, will be familiar to your lips, and the past seven weeks at sea – an unfamiliar rite of passage – will have been worth it. The day is May 23, 1914, and the ship that carries your dreams is named the *Komagata Maru*.

When the ship's anchor drops, your eyes draw to the rising land mass known as North Vancouver. Awake. Awoken. The dawn plays tricks on your eyes. You see shapes taking form, colossal shapes, square shapes hulked over the harbour. But your mind sees your farm as it was in your boyhood, before you took your place in the British Armed Forces and before serving the British Raj, where you wagered and worked war in the Sudan, in Somaliland, in China, and at Saragarhi, on behalf of your master. You remember the corn, rice, red peppers, and sugar cane at the farm, knowing the same force that drives the roots down into your fields also brings the season's meaning and is infused in your body.

You wonder why Mathaji sold two parcels of your land for you to journey to this new place, why your family still could not afford to keep you, without sending you away into a world unknown. And the remaining two parcels of sugar cane you harvested turn into income for the local government; the vizier, the sarpanch, the British civil servant.

Not knowing how much you were impoverished by your master. That the drain on your country of Bharat cost your home 1 billion pounds sterling over a 50-year period; or that during that time, 19 million people died of famine while Bharat paid England's debt at about 244 million pounds in 1900, with annual increases since then; or that nearly 105 million pounds drained away every year from India without a penny's return. You do not know the compounded interest amounting to 72.5 million pounds increased India's famine, not drought or overpopulation. Awful poverty was caused by the largest foreign tribute ever seen, matched by an equally expensive tribute to the Indian durbars, royal families who squandered your labour and livelihood.

This letter is to you, my friend, because you are not awake to your sacrifice to the greatest of endeavours: freedom, as you try to find ways out of the complete poverty of your arrival in the new land and the living poverty at home on the farm.

You will not know these things because these points of light have not been shone in your eyes. You are the unwilling participant in an event that once again gives birth to the idea of freedom and self-determination in your homeland; the idea, not the death of the *Maru*!

You place your foot up onto the gangplank and look to feel the earth again under your feet. Voices from the shoreline shout out to you, "Keep off the land" or "Drive the beggars back to the Ganges." You comply, seventy years have seeped into your actions, your thoughts – you comply with every demand and order meted out by the British, even here. You step back and take your place amongst the others and await the next move.

In front of you is the ship's charterer who convinced you in Singapore that life in Canada will be one of good living. Gurdit Singh asks the shore man: "Immigration Inspector Malcolm Reid, why the delay?" Reid replies: "The whole boat will be quarantined for medical checkups, and following that, each individual on the ship will have to have $200 in his pocket and be travelling direct passage from his place of birth." (Implausible since there are no ships travelling non-stop from India to Vancouver, Canada.) You step back, deprived of community and wait out a medical checkup that will last over ten days, as opposed to the customary twenty-four-hour check.

The rations on the ship diminish in the following fortnight. Day turns into day and the ship becomes Vancouver's mobile penned zoo. By this time a three-shift watch consisting of two armed police guards will keep an eye on your every move, as you slowly descend into yourself and feel your whole world squeezed into this ship. When asked for food by Gurdit Singh,

Inspector Reid states it is Gurdit Singh's responsibility to feed the passengers, knowing Singh cannot move or acquire funds for foods.

Trying to land in Canada, you have been denied your humanity. Stories are written about you that never reach your eyes or ears, yet they provoke the rising cries and anger that drift from the wharf, slip into the water to surround and crawl up against the ship and ricochet off the ship into the lifeboats and steel cables that hang above your head.

The Vancouver *Sun* runs stories saying "the right-thinking people know that the natives of Hindustan ... should not be allowed in this country, except for circus purposes ... We do not think as Orientals do. That is why the East Indians and other Asiatic races and the white race will always mis-comprehend each other ..." or "The Sikhs are like the Irish raised to the nth or fourth dimension. They are remorseless politicians and disturbers. They are complex and quite unaccountable ... For the sake of the picturesque I am glad to have a few specimens. But those who came last (on the *Komagata Maru*) are not quite up to the sample. They must be returned as such." On your behalf, there are those in the Indo-Canadian press who applaud your arrival. *The Hindustanee* paper published by Husain Rahim: "We extend a cordial welcome to Bhai Gurdit Singh and his party of 375 East Indians on board the *Komagata Maru* which arrived in this harbour.

All kinds of spectacular and alarming stories in which the arrival of this ship has been termed a Hindu invasion have been indulged in by the local press day after day in their sensation mongering dailies, while the Empress boat, bringing 650 Chinese at the same time, was welcome ..."

In a week, after days of negotiations for food, you will have received provisions, but in the height of summer, you will parch, as the fresh water supply runs out on the ship. Amid the politics of whether the community of South Asians living in Vancouver should foot the bill, or whether the government who has imprisoned you as innocent people on the ship should foot the bill, your mouth runs dry and you drink "bad dirty water, in which you become sick with cough and throat sores." When the fouled water is finished, you will have to wait until the politics subside, and Inspector Reid – having accepted and then deferred his legal responsibility – gives the City of Vancouver the legal choice of deciding whether your devalued life is worth helping under the Public Charges Act.

The surrounding faces will tell you all. You are cramped in filth in a rundown cargo ship without drinking water, with few food items.

On Dominion Day, the shoreline is packed with onlookers crowding the harbour and you are both spectacle and recreation. You are left with one meal a day of potato soup and rice, leaving no water supply.

By July 9, to salvage Reid's public image, you are supplied rations that will last a few days. Hunger drones day by day. The battles you fought will not equal the misery and degradation that is now your life in the New World.

The Battle of Burrard Inlet will not begin with your actions and will not end with your surrender. On July 19, at 1:30 a.m., the assault begins against the beaten body of the old *Maru*. Through hunger, thirst, and filth, you look for what would defend you from the state terrorism that prevails upon the scene. With firebrick, pieces of machinery, hatchets, coal, iron bars, and makeshift clubs, you defend yourself against a piercing stream from firehoses, and you know shots echo in your ears and across the water. The night report stated that you had a pistol yet they decided not to use gunfire.

You succeed in one thing: to be victorious in one battle for the freedom and equal movement as a citizen of the British Empire. You become a martyr for the cause, though your eventual journey to imprisonment and death still awaits across forty-six changing waters. Defenceless, still a pauper, you will see from the distance a warship coming your way. The HMCS *Rainbow* arriving at 8:15 in the morning anchors two hundred yards away from your freighter. The *Rainbow*'s arsenal consists of two six-inch and six four-inch torpedo tubes. The ammunition supply consists of old-fashioned shells. The tubes are aimed directly at your head. Along with this is the Vancouver Militia, including the Sixth Regiment and the Irish Fusiliers and Highlanders. In your freight, all you have is coal. The whole of Vancouver will be out to see your demise as their morning's entertainment.

With Punjabi lives laid down for the British Armed Forces, does the lunar light cut across the wave and linger on in your mind? A question asked out of exasperation sparks the heart of revolution; once an ally and now the enemy.

Dr. Oscar Douglas Skelton writes to Sir Wilfrid Laurier: "This nucleus of the new Canadian navy was first used to prevent British subjects from landing on British soil."

The *Maru* drifts out to sea at 5:00 a.m. on July 23, 1914. You have provisions, your sleep eases, but the final sacrifice awaits you at Budge Budge, India, where as a perceived criminal you will lay down your life as 177 rounds of .303 bore from the Royal Fusiliers pierce your group.

Dreams dissipate as these arteries spill over and a massacre's only witness is the rippling waves of the Hooghly River.

I offer this one last piece of information in your memory from an anonymous quote – dated January 5, 1914:

"What good has India done us? First it has increased the small island of England to the largest empire in the world, and has given them wisdom, strength and happiness. I will tell you the benefits one by one. All the regiments have been formed from India. All our merchant ships steaming in all ports of the world have been built by the wealth of India. All the big buildings in London are built out of Indian money. If it were not for India, England would be unknown today. The modern towns of Edinburgh, Cheltenham, and Bath have all been built with Indian money. It was by the help of the Indian merchants and Indian money that we were enabled to fight Napoleon Bonaparte. It was only by the help of Indian money that we were enabled to defeat and bind him and deport him to an island in the Atlantic Ocean. These benefits have been done for England by India, but the Indian people are not aware of their strength."

Vancouver, British Columbia, 2014

a ship's story

i was born
in the yards of scotstoun shipyard
    launched into the clyde river and given a german name
        the straight funnel of my body
            threaded skyward by taut cables webbing heaven bound
        my body a glory of black steel

            i moved at the fastest pace then
        i am old now and my sojourn near the end

for this voyage my new master
    purchased a second life for me

                the old world exhausted me
                I had already made more than ninety-two crossings
                between two worlds

                in the new world my usefulness was extinguished

                tomorrow i will become the parts of the sum
                feeding the salt water the debris that was my body

    each part of me i will offer to the unloved
        in hope my wards will be made complete
            whole for another life
                while my life escapes me

if you were to admire me, then
    do so when I was beautiful and strong
        do so when my name was young
do so even now as i return the unloved
    delivering them to the rifles, lathis, and jails of britain's bharat

diese störrisch haken

"she was delivered to the German company dampfschiffs rhederei hansa of hamburg, and was registered under the name SS Stubbenhuk. *She was subsequently acquired by the Hamburg America Line of Germany, where she sailed as the SS* Sicilia *from 1894"*

we move backward against the clock on the high tide

our destination my new life

on the quiet waters that kiss the bank of the elbe

i understand now my body will carry the world

the river swallows me whole

into commerce

we arrive as the day passes into evening

the port city's hand before me

a sepal of fingers close in

as my guide threads me through

this bulbous foci of business

water ways thick with human capital

the port opens up to me

the wharf and each berth a perfection of design

my body slowly eases into my transient home

my nautical journey just now beginning

those looking for respite will be my friend

i will carry each burden

for tomorrow and the days after

ten anonymous journeys

coal clouds and gulls hang steady in the wind
songs, scuffles, shuffles, screams, receipts

paper ways of mean

dream arteries surge seaward
pistons beat, engines screech
and a cacophonous wind thunders

barnacled black hulls slice and sluice out
through the streaming scheldt from antwerp

the port delivers the coal and cargo
erosions ripple over memory
slip the border
lost in the rip
of tide

they feed the loss
my body brims and bleeds into the thick air against the atlantic

sisters, brothers, cousins, and great ancestors pass in quiet

————   masters schmidt and theiles,
eye the violence in the waters
the flap clap wind shifts
a pattern
the deep distance, the long droning notes of my lungs

————   we curl into the confluence of the labrador
breaking through contrarian waves

          my hulled hands crash against the tide   —————
to the unloved I will offer

a part of me
       in hope my wards will be made complete

     for another life

          —————

        while my indentured life escapes me
admire me then
   do so when
this beauty subsides
     when my name ages
        do so when i transmute, shift my name
        and become the ss *komagata maru*

my name is *sicilia*, you called me saviour once

(rusted tin box found snagged at the end of the
Wakkanai North Seawall, Hokkaido, Japan, in 1995)

Archival Note: # KM file 10038 - hks95 - Contents Revealed:
Item inside the box - sealed letter - opened and entered as record

"for tomorrow then, and the days after February 9, 1926"

to my friend ellis

ellis, my friend, you have a rotund capacity for irony
you are kind enough to remember me from before
sometimes you listen to my weariness

if you were to ask the question who they were
then i would tell you clearly who they were

russian and ukrainian families swathed in scarves
patriarchs with stiff straw hats and hard eyes
families escaping the unspoken pogroms, losing their old names

solitary greek and italian boy-men
ready-made labourers walking into tomorrow's progress
in the corner end of a new york   moment

anchorless unknown citations misidentified – women, men, and other
always an invitation to invention and lineage

young women, eyes glisten against
the spectacle of arrival, departure, and arrival

the emptied-out lives of the recently widowed and orphaned
one remaining family member
leaving behind graves and grave names with no bodies
while deep in the hills, the mouldering ash marks a dead disease

whole reconstructed families
find the dark hull the last sanctuary
rusted and ready
homes on stone pavements

the smoking walls of marsovan
evacuated homes
dust prints toward the desert
the trek that conjured up dreams of bayonets, axes, execution
names removed from lives, silence brought to lips
an erasure of neighbourhoods during the summer heat

each loved survivor arrived in le havre, samsun, smyrna
stepped into my body
papers full with fiction and fact
names true and less true
anonymous and deceased ones now with new life

and those who survived
agopian, fenerdjian, malhassian, mardikian, tcoulian …
a manifest ship laden with fact, fiction, and forgetting

one, or more
lost, driven
seeking solace
of an emptied mind
tear ducts swollen
salt water
for the journey

on arrival at the centre many replied
"… no thnich … no thni city"
… *blank*
gained amnesia
disembarked

into a future

thirty-four thousand, one hundred and twenty-four

34,124

the redness of things

six hands with scarlet fingers

    dusk

        shape shifts turning crimson at night

    a martyr chooses the dark path to the gallows

        sanguinary and precise

the horizon steeped in a rust-filled sunset
    seeps into the quiet waters

        today will be yesterday and the world will be tomorrow
          and future unfolds without my hand

        the hull now dusted with an orange swath of pocked skin
        scab flakes trail in the cliffed ridges of the after   · wave

"I can only surmise that the instructions from the
Department at Ottawa to the Immigration authorities here
was to delay matters and procrastinate and delay until
such time as these people were starved back to their
original port from when they sailed."
                        – J.E. Bird, June 1914

subedhar, sub alt din, alter-sub-alt-in
sub alt urn

"Public opinion in this country will not tolerate
immigration in any considerable number from Asiatic
countries and that even more drastic measures and
regulations will, if necessary, be provided in order to
prevent any influx of Hindus."
– Prime Minister Robert Borden to
Hon. G.H. Perley, High Commissioner
to Great Britain, July 17, 1914

deep within my body, a yellow tongue licks the wall
the floor, the beds, and the cramped benches
and moves over the unloved who slumber each day

deep within my body a babe sniffles
drinking the nutrition out of her mother

deep within my body a young boy wonders …
his mother holds his hand tightly and weeps

deep within my body fauja singh dreams
of an ocean and scaling mountains

deep within my body a doctor coughs
seeing that his oath will mean nothing here
his educated fears seeking safety on all sides

deep within my body, men become darkness itself
their smiles suffocate on barren stomachs

in the deep darkness where no one sleeps
fear and ignorance consume each other
and madness settles in
to sleep and love

(psalms) to the four clergy

*"I would like four Christian Clergymen to talk to me, and
I will show them from my holy book that the action I have
taken to right this wrong is in that book ..."*
— Court Proceedings, Testimony of Mewa Singh,
New Westminster, 1915

i walk the four corners of life
where there are three places of absence
my name is wrought in the language of solitude
where the dawn meets king edward
the smell of cedar and sawdust are my comforts

the touch of my cotton is a half-centimetre away from the cloth of your lord

each morning the day's arc meets me halfway
each path is my thin straight line between meaning and unmeaning
each day i write my life in the margins of my faith
each sunday i enter the walls of my gurus
at the house of meaning
silence seeps into me
each day i hear the cackle of judgment
amid the close quarters of each day's work
each hour my silence is the rain drenching cobblestones

*these hours of back and forths
is this the nowhere spot
the absent place
the cavernous eye
as the distant crackling light stabs across
the sky
while the thunder moans around us*

*what bleeds into the confluence of these
interests*

to the four clergy

i am a man between friends
my teacher returns to ash
the architect was draped with a flag last week
your city mourns him
and i await the gallows
the knot of my destiny awaits me
my pinched esophagus constricts without mourning

"I shall gladly have the rope put around my neck thinking it to be a rosary of God's name ..."

my dead hands will carry my burdens in hulled silence
as this town carries its sadness when the winter rains fall
quiet faces   downward glancing
i am a murderer in your eyes   i walk with intention

. – .
. – .
. – .

ship man
i fess

                                    passengers

                                              listing

this stubborn hook 1892 1893 1894

ship manifest and passenger listing

                    sicilia
                  1894
                 1895
                  1896
                   1897
                    1898
                     1899
                      1900
                     1901
                    1902
                   1903
                  1904
                 1905
                1906
               1907

i am at the ocean's feet considering the desolation in waves
we are speaking of our past, and the burden of love
my virtual hands hulled around a record

To settle the prairies, Sifton vigorously wooed American farmers, people from Scotland and the North of England, and Eastern and Central European peasants. He believed that only agriculturalists and peasants made desirable settlers.

"When I speak of quality I have in mind, I think, something that is quite different from what is in the mind of the average writer or speaker upon the question of Immigration. I think a stalwart peasant in a sheep-skin coat, born on the soil, whose forefathers have been farmers for ten generations, with a stout wife and a half-dozen children, is good quality."

– Sir Clifford Sifton

Koma / Komāsharu – singular reference to commercial activity; *gata / kata* – suffix to pluralize pronoun within a polite and neutral usage – multiple commercial activities; *maru* – beloved, a formal affectation designated to a ship by the captain or senior officer); *komagata maru* in its literal Japanese usage means "beloved ship protecting the respected commercial activities of the proprietor"

it is with regret and sadness that seafarer *heian maru* (previously known as the *komagata maru, sicilia,* and *stubbenhuk*) passed away off the coast of cape sōya, hokkaido, japan, on february 11, 1926. she is the sole member of her family and has no siblings. none of her remains were retrieved from the sea and it is believed that at the age of 36 her body began to disintegrate and parts of her were taken under the local currents and may have drifted to other parts of the island network and beyond through other currents to the west coast u.s. states of oregon, washington, and alaska, and the canadian province of british columbia

during her life, she played a significant role in the lives of 34,124 persons who sought sanctuary and a new path in the new world. without her determination and resourcefulness, many would have not made it so easily to their destinations and new homes

in her later years she was the subject of much international intrigue as more than 376 individuals sought her assistance in helping them to gain a new life in british columbia. as the *komagata maru* carried them for more than five months and housed them while they remained in maritime captivity and became victims of starvation and unsanitary conditions. this event is her one final, personal tragedy in that she was not able to successfully and safely see these sojourners become permanent residents of their newly adopted homeland

more recently a found letter dated to 1926 illuminates a life lived in service and highlights a melancholy for the work that was not completed, and the one issue that was never resolved or reconciled, for attached to this letter is a poetic piece called *a ship's story*

condolences can be made through an act of kindness. the *maru* would have wanted it this way

breeze (a story)

interview fragment logged by detaining officer Constable Macuard dated
August 14, 1999 (canine unit interpreter services offered but declined)

, *breeze knew english*

"… the invitation
        came from a man
                with a serpentine face
                        his tongue pointing upward taking in the air as he smiled

it was a discount deal
            you know my meaning
                        free room and roaming
                                    free passage to salivate

    my culinary life was an exploration in decay
find a meal was my goal

i explored, i walked, and i ran
                my coat will tell you of my impurity
                        it is as rich as poverty
                                my mother bore me into this
                    my ribs protruded outward as I lay against her nipple
                        my mother was born here, my father in wuyishan
                            my father was away a lot in other gullies

leaving my nanchang jie squat

i carry no distinctive features that might endear me to you

the canal with its putrid pitch pushing forward
                remains by my side
                        heat waves pull up the fetid fumes
                            dwelling deep in the viscous mass

            lining the canal
        gnawed cuts of rank offal, cartilage, and carcass
crowd the drain

my guardian was like me
no distinctions, withered, a slight desperation in his gait
his dark eyes looking downward
constant in their search, they glisten toward everything

we met at the confluence of nothing
the air a mélange of diesel, rank cooking oil
the acute crisp smell of the dead

their quiet presence always in my nostrils

an array shadows
the path to his home is similar to the path
gullies and unplanned sewers and waterways of my last dwelling
sunlight sharp and slivered splashed on a muddied linoleum patch
the serpentine man approached me while i loitered
my life was valued at forty yuan, given to a stranger for no reason
she stared at me for a while
looked into her palm, was about to say something but turned away

mr. serpentine put a collar on me
          six hands carried me and threw me into a ruinous cage
            the lock a bare click, the bars all brown and red
              my new dwelling a little bigger than my body

             the cage was placed onto a listing ship

from sea to sun

"... will detain the arrivals for uncertain identity, it is likely that this will not be sustainable as experience shows that most Sri Lankans are able to establish their identity in a timely manner."

scuppers bleed rust water into the pacific
        a red-clad body hulls sideways
                breaking a fall onto the top deck
                      her jeans scuff marked
              the water of human cargo dribbles
lower decks teem with humid enclosure
bilge-brown rivulets roaming to the sun and sea
on the waterline, the salt kiss never ends

let's play another game today, gamini – i want you to imagine the deck is your home and that your cousins aadhi and vena are with you and you have decided to play the word game. remember to explain the word clearly, and make sure aadhi and vena explain theirs too ... yes ... i know, you played this one a week ago ... we will reach there soon and I will bring you many new games

        it is a flexible approach
        this rough and tough
        it allows for collaboration
        agency co-operation
        a flexible triage is today's way
let's just make sure we don't co-opt each other
        quarantine plans – check
        medical checks – check
        masks – check
        identification and interview questions – check
        detention and site security – check
        individual case management procedures – check
        executive oversight and execution – check
        implementation execution – check

        we begin

let's play another game, gamini, your favourite, the fill-me ga-me

you play a young child and medical patient with no nutrients left
i will be the mother who was bled dry of everything
you will wear the mask and carry your ruined birth certificate
I will play ... what we saw when we left home
you will play the wounds aadhi and vena carried
this time both of us will play two actors playing innocents fleeing the crime
scene
tomorrow,
we play mourners of your cousins and their parents who were my siblings
today we play so-journers together looking for home

mama, who are they with the navy-blue shirts and pants
our saviours

mama, who are we
gamini, today we are refugees

dereliction suite

i.

these words
a centrifugal dereliction

two-tiered
air-conditioned
class appropriate

words
on a bench
orange peel
dimpled skinned fingers
forefinger
essence
around
nail biting
into trajectory
flesh

sweat blinding
drips across
dark sockets
falling into the cavernous O
where oracles once lived

convalescing quietly
out of chaos
obliviated
shaded out
lined up against the far wall
charcoal clouds drift
into a pale concrete gutter

my mind a rectangle
cramped encas(t)ement
breathing heavy
i'm heavy ... i'm feeling
breathing heavy
with freedom
incline into solitude

ii.

weary wandering wilderness leap
sinister pacific waves
consume rusted-out shells
sweating flesh
cascades
along waters bordered
landed
border
residence
sewn
stitched
crackled
scaly
colourless
skin

trains perpendicular
to boundaries
barbed-wire fences
cauldrons of water and rice
encamp the derelict
clean 'em
licked for discarding
sequestered arms
negotiating tight spaces

to say someday
i will sway and dance with you
along tight, lined heat
glistening with war
circle the centre
reck / tangle
this trivia

this day's interest
tomorrow's ambivalence
a national distrust

capture the half-smile
crease it and tear up the corners
until it is a full frown

make it your own

antennae of invisible skin

nodes of knowing

a stranded molecule

e. coli races for infection

does amnesia capture

the pathology of silence

M.R.J.R. /EC.

Vancouver, 30 June 8th

W. D. SCOTT, ESQ.,

Superintendent of Immigration,

Ottawa, Ont.

Sir:-

I beg to confirm my night lettergram of the 6th
instant, as follows:-

"Message forwarded Governor General Ottawa tonight,
begins, Reference Province sixth reply to your enquiry
Immigration Agent untrue. Reid never supplied anything
still starving. Officials made search fourth, found
no provisions treating cruelly appoint commission for
investigation? Reply paid ten words. Signed Passengers
Komagata Maru. Message ends. Medical Inspector Monroe
visited ship today and offered to take ship's Doctor
(Hindu) ashore, but Gurdit Singh refused permit him to
ashore to obtain medicines although representations
has been made to me same were urgently needed."

Also my night lettergram of the 7th instant, as follows:-

"Gurdit Singh has tonight wired the Governor General
as follows. Begins, Governor General, Ottawa. Reid
disallowed my landing; have coal cargo to sell cant
take more cargo; suffering heavy losses and starvation.
Charter money eleven thousands bound to pay before
eleventh. Cant arrange unless go ashore otherwise lose
ship. Government responsible of damage. Reid disallow
conversation with anybody; given many notices, no re-
sponse. Charterer, Komagata Maru. Ends. Patrol Boat
Winnimac in commission tonight for first time. "

Your obedient servant,

Malcolm. R. J. Reid

DOMINION IMMIGRATION AGENT & INSPECTOR.

beloved ships without war

memory

i will bring you hope and safety

you will return home without harm

beloved ships without war

memory

i will bring you hope and safety

you will return home without harm

from fragments

wisconsin temple poems

temple the prayer

the sun tips the high top of surreal
page the turner
book revelates
heart spreads outward
the mind
semi-automatic
life a 9 mm cycle
the caved-out soul empty as
sockets
arm to hand
hand to arm
eleven spoken for nine
six ways to bless the chosen ones
and the sun runs high into the day

you are constant in each and every heart, and in all things.

some give, some beg, this your wondrous play

you
the one who walks beside
you

a found profile re-profiled

veterans day baby
forty
an arm nine-one-one'd
armed force psych op 1992
patterns of misconduct
honourable discharge
criminal misdemeanours – dui and missed chief
bass playing to belong ... to something ... anything
practise the target
"other" the regalia of
input image here

...

investigative erasure

200

300

200

40

6

acted alone

not assisted

200

investigative leads, 300

interviews, more than 200

pieces of evidence

the results of its expansive investigation

no evidence was uncovered

no evidence to suggest

ongoing threat

the sikh community

the attack was part of any ongoing threat to the sikh community."

to conclude this attack was … directed or facilitated by any white

supremacist group.

during the shooting at the temple, page exchanged gunfire with two

oak creek police officers seriously wounding one, before being shot by

another officer, then turning his weapon on himself.

a sikh temple in oak creek

police perspective on his motives consisted of four sentences

yet when the federal bureau of investigation announced why

wade michael page, 40, killed six people at

"the fbi investigation indicates wade michael page acted alone and was not

assisted in committing this violent crime killing six and wounding four

other victims," the fbi's statement said in november

mourning ghazals

i.

five leather fingers outward answer, blessed without
the debris, its arc reaching a dome without

grace, crackling yellow phosphorescent tear to sear
swift curve script against pale plaster wall without

flags of dead skin draped over broken stones
fossils proselytized for future posterity, a prayer without

mourners, the silhouetted fragments in the dry wind
a shadow in the sun's shimmer left without

ii.

this other cactus land, the other straw men
this azure seduction of two orthodoxies without

three epidermal layers on pale-brown dawn
history's class lesson is a million half-truths without

a tempest stillborn lost from the skeletal hand
the crimson river downward driven without

pupil, paper-thin fingernails on site of learning
blindness bled to escape one horror, a sight without

iii.

wormed soil sandwiched between clay
a murmur, the small spring, weary arms lift without

arched finger upward, one question offered to a final prophet
two fingers answer to supplicate, the body supine without

facing east of station, the bustle of product placement
tragedy water-fronted, rail and weighed through benign everydays without

the flat palm an exasperated call to daily prayer
echoes ricochet from the prayer mat never weaved to be without

iv.

place, on cool grey pools of concrete, industrial lineage
beaten orange thread entreats the beloved without

clean sheen of answer and to emulate and ape
a mirror tells you who is the fairest of all, but without

a microphone prayer, a precise oration, the art of awe
to shine from those who never live … without

hands splayed, imploding phoenix careening toward peace
this body chapped, another geography corroded, without

v.

skin in dry heat, the armless ghost walks
vipers hissing in the wind, vacated eyes without

snug embrace, a red drill dribbles down the frontal lobe, like lava
khoon does that sometimes, seducing to slumber without

the embedded life exit, to join the ghoul and spook
look into each other's eyes, *ambiguate*, walk without

the oratory mouth agape will almost say
"this ...
    i ...
          not ...
                end ...
                      this ...
                            without ..."

vi.

the distraction and gnawing synapse spasm
starvation, hunger, heroin

the wet mind shivers in the arid dream
the muffled glass gaze will continue without

the hand ... the arm ... the supplicant body
now dried and caked, the unspoken mind without

its soul, the ephemeral breath in twilight brush
dry leaves scraping the dead well without

this ghazal a deformed wail to the sky
this makta breath evaporates, an erasure of name without ...

3 flag poems – dry skin draped over clay stones

i.

hours become catapults off the cadaver
each heat wave full on a slow wind
smoke-filled, crackling luminous night
blankets the twilight
as if someone said

you will not bind yourself

to love

today

ii.

the currents mourn
mother's caress carcasses
the patter breaks on the brown haze
hands that do not move
held

the yellow milk drips
into the red sand

iii.

would dorothy still be loved

had they flown in on a tide of precision

her friends

      lion   *   →

             tin man   *   →

                         man of straw   *   →

would they be loved?

the rivers

"u-freight"   war with ease
the tigris

arteries between worlds
kernels rolling in the hot wind
swallowed by sand

there was no fifth finger on the baby

alone the man known as alex stood up
between the rivers
his arms a world of numbers and signs
hands pushing out to stop time

whispering

what have I done?

the dead carried the young
buried them deep
the sandstorm swallowed everything

ants

when the cavalry came

each one raised antennae to dead skin

drank up death

touched a last remaining thought

from
the
limp
leg
they
jumped
and
circum
navigated
up
the
pole

a
dark
line
ascending

in
search
of
murder

each spine node
flattened
across
the
bridge's
path

what convinces the mind to run and rail in chaos?

to bend sanity like a loose thought

desert

lives through a body's con
tour

a home reno

rendered

a rendition renditioned

        as charcoal
        precipice

ishtar
lights up the sky
a haze of yellow phosphorescence

bowed and aimed
heaven tilts the tears
shooting toward the thick-cliffed sand

i with i
palmed upward

fingers

seek

grace

emancipate this word and a perilous friend

this sinewy revolution

suave as
self
myth

touch truth
        reference truth

        be

        told

        leave the facts

        behind
footsteps

clap away

toward the distance

atomic eeyore

okay

thanks for thinking of me

if you want me to

you know

they forgot one horse

okay

i'm not a horse

but if i were

i would ride from a blue sky

undoing what my cousins started

today i'm in the desert

screaming when night becomes day

my master vaporized

thanks for thinking of me

i've been following ordered verse again

smile

i want to sew on a smile
stitch a blood thread

dark and muddy
ingest bleach
for my new home

it will wash away the coloured hue of my story
i will carry a note with a promise
pledge myself to a new name
mute a haunting scream
that carries over my mind

ask my guru to offer a morning blessing
a thumb print of ash
contours mapping the middle point
on my forehead

i might leave you if you desire me no more
remain silent
agree that solitude is beautiful
fingers and hand gently caress my mouth

x   x'd mouth
xxx

my history a quarrel

a long starched thread

never allowed to curl

chita – 100 lines to die

a prince a boy

dream

if only

this moment

was a folkloric moment

repeated one ounce

at a time

stand still

reach for

a special, weekly, daily feudal moment

pride measured in a hundred special collections

one *buda*, two *shoté*
ounces, not kilos
never that
never made
for anything

a fifteen-second mug-shot moment
tattoo arm
double sword
arrow arm

double-edged truth
cleaved
to begin

> we sway in quiet conspiracy
> unable to tell the truth

double-edged destiny
a silence before shame

catch the sun's ray
it sets without a heaven

behind the *chunee*
a mother stands beside the drapes
a silhouette brown
alienates

divine knowledge
this *miri* moment
in the absence of *piri*
a father's manic smile
in the midst of a double mortgage
fears his own skin

rakhri

in two months
a red thread
circled around wrist
diminishes

it takes him years
to dissolve
            devolve
transform
expire
and aspire

takes two months
to push the packs
packed
minute
to the hour
on the intersection
of white light
the thoroughfare
of deal
it is four months of biz
before he realizes he
betrayed her

the world after tomorrow

presence

a room brims
with ideas
we catch
scratch back
step back

consider another weave
and "other" narrative
each broken piece, our soul healed
by the iridescent fall light

walk toward no conclusion
or pronouncement

to drift in silence to the floor of the maple tree in late autumn
un-owned nor repatriated
dreaming toward its own veined humanity

both are inexplicably linked

grandmother's soft and fleshy palm
placed on forehead
her head tipped forward brushes against your brow
offers a word
jhindé raeho
continue to live

hollow

we speak solitude

a silky self-reflexive smile
imprint

shift
places

trade

a lulled repetition

familiar smile
manic eye

> *my world ends*
> *when you do that*

the numbness shifts you into sleep

> *i say i love you*

> *i know*

> *i say i want happiness*

> *i try*

i say i want, i want to say, i want and say

to live through this with you

you say … i hh- … no … we've had a hard time with it

moments recede
iris constricts again
the mud path pupil dilates
this dark hour flourishes
crinkled plum leaves drape across my shoulders
i make a poor king for it

waves

curl against the sand
water cresting
your roaring proclamation arrives

i watch you leave the world
violent legs snap against foam
limp weeds stick to your thighs
pushing you farther away
broad-shouldered neck creased in crucifixion

a thin line rolling up
against you
away from
my gaze

the sleek lines
of the young
crash against currents
movie-star gestures by everyday faces
branded moms dads children

you mark anger in each plunge
your own silent victory
our children drift toward you
their umbilical yearning
even now you feed them
gather them
return with them to the water
to a place where they began

and i watched

dawn

dawn's cool breath on your cactus palm

brushes over prickled finger

lover, you slept alone when warmth flew away into night

parched, you look away

the trouble with directions are

they visit both of us

3:00 a.m.

knuckles drawn into 3:00 a.m.

a moonless night

spine settles deep into a rain-cloud floor

windows of sorrow

reflect the kitchen light

a jittering silhouette

of a still figure looking outward

sleep walking

i hear the murmur

the blade scratching against the throat
curved toes
arched high
an imprint on a leaf

toward the dawn

... breathe

... breathe

pencil thought

caress the rib of an hb light

charcoal the mist to preface the morning

circumnavigate this septic-ular thought

each echo arches high and sits there in the frontal lobe

crackling leaves

feet walking backward toward the dawn light

ash

if i bathed you in silk
threw jasmine petals warm from the sun
onto you
will you be blessed?

you sleep in beauty
my body clay and bone
you the sky
the warm rays blanket your closed lids
you hurl me back to earth

recline in a cedar box
hot flames to gather you full
hot will you be carried
hot will you be

a small crimson ash
curls inward
glows and dis

        appears

we both drifted into sleep

return

your life
a bay window
scratch marks on the back
of your hand
the love
you seek
the world's contours
it will only scar you
from within

long uncreased fingers
your maternal arms
anonymous
dreams, you linger
you asked *where did I go …*

a touch soft
a rough touch
inflected moment
two mirrors
these eyes invite
and yearn for
self

swing

indigo swing
   flow
   shift
   flutter

across sacred side
ways glance

   check ... wait
   strike light in hand

mystical application
phoneme.syllable.metonym
contiguous passage

   birth reduces us

     a ♀

  ♂ riffs a spoken
       word

 love rebounds
 ricochets

   your life tips fingers outward
   watches you begin ... end ... begin

   swing

how this music returns

asiancy (a word) *(for r.m.)*

in form
past
present

reflect before an act

reconcile, reconciliation

repair the broken

blazing a path in the midst of enemies, even your own kind

your feet stationary / parallel perfect
the military precision of a high brick wall looming over you
invisible ink stains, words written over hard red clay
from those who almost spoke to the bricks and mortar
bowed their heads in quiet and turned eastward
their destination, the blurred outline of the unknown

seeking a chip in the concrete

a moment
where
the crack opens and shifts a little

finding the weak spot, or if not the weak spot

walking the long path around that wall

patience

empathy

seeking
that slight scrape
the sound of the emancipation door

a race through while knowing the race is rigged

rigging another paradigm to equate civil rights to the living world

watching for the light, always watching for the light

chardi kala
the finest art in life is victory over oppression

grace

this silence
this lamp
this language
upon the dark path

it illuminates

of friends

a deck shuffle of outdated biz cards this way

your magic trick   that way

sleight of hand

on where   your intent went

being relative   is a lifestyle choice

the voice track   what says and does not say

a dramatic laugh   through tightened lips

bravado   bravo

a hemming way   a victory kind of way

our false dance   that glorious moment

speak   around the truth

one look askance

thinking

how did we end up next to a dumpster

after tomorrow

two empty homes
two men sitting in darkness
one relieved it is over
catching his breath-filled failures
his scuffle over the phone
when vulnerability sets in
the rough distance breathes and quietly
seeps in

between f(r)owned words
hands crack and crease

stand and still searching
the small-walled dents
dust settled in corners
the absent lover's embrace
the memory
quiet times within quiet houses

abandonment
the weakness of gender
anonymous patrolling eye

denial in birthday pictures of a son

open doors punish
barren rooms mock with cracked plaster
rooms expect nothing from nothing
the calamitous baby yearns
the absent smell
even the outreach for a hand
close the fist
hoping the full circle is unbroken

illusory beginnings eluding incarcerated thoughts
or to move this other silence between
us

the simple line around the circumference
how everything warms with voice
living in rooms
cold and enraged
the manic voice that keeps
rat-a-tat-tatting on a migrant mind

seeking forgiveness
not for the silence
or what was said

because the path is a hollowed-out mountain
lives lived too many times
amid these high walls
the bitter green moss in mouths
that fall on so many times
before we could break

the range

grief

six eyes couched

looked out

as the ashen clouds reached into them

scarved their hearts

breathed a cold wet kiss into them

and muddied their minds

one hand reached for a luminous line

one hand tucked the hair behind the ear

all were searching for the six eyes that left

sadness

then the plates empty

we talk of burden

pulling a weight

of responsibility

our bodies slow

deliberate

the lip of expectation

and this bearing of news

a transitive moment

between dream

and the living

it-dhé (here), a vancouver special circa 1980

you could say
      the brass fittings
      on my double front door
are a *namasthe* to the west side
sat sri akal to the southlands

and that
      the baked white
      smart-slabbed path
writes a perpendicular   L
to my home

tread quietly then
      the sleeping basement
      has the sun high above
the chalk-walled room's mustard air
absorbs the slumber

in a cloud of human failings
      mattress on the floor
      double mattress in the bedroom
couch cover bulbous
with rose design

scrapes sleeping skin
      the day's discordant music
      the broken bitten words of night
the childhood echo
a sad man's dream
awakes   again

melancholy

the small curling wave slapping the sand
the undulating sisters following forward
into death
two young knees with feet splayed
the thigh against the absence that was a lover

slate-grey rain bouncing off the ground
i can do this i can do this i can change
a theorem
a regimen
a yoga mat
a double dosage of the placebo that was given last year
clothes that hug and fawn
mirrors and light that kiss the wounded
as they continue their bond
two tapering worms ringing themselves along the stem of needles
the long sigh exhaled from the misjudged observer

the unrequited and unanswered kiss
that drove the unloved to despair
a heart empties into rawness

rough hands of the ringed fingers cleaning pine scent off
a hotel mirror
a restaurant mirror
an office toilet mirror

the closed door of the four minds
the closure of chemical movement
solitude
a deathly synapse

yellow ovals of light blink
and slick over
inked water
film and foam
filtering pale
over distant waters

the laugh of young children around a bonfire at night
the memory
of a bonfire
two young children laughing

autumn drift

red stem embarks upon cool breeze
an inner music lilts
how sound waves pan over palm
a leaf over velvet hand
dry embrace
a famished embrace
yet the music feeds

in conversation

re-word

since

here

ear

ere

hear in

sin

nine

sinched

here

sin in insin

s.o.s.

soma

mai mai

r.e.m.

I'm so sin-surr

slam

i am the subject
of
a pervading
long-term
anonymously applied denouement

    a free fall freestyle real time limbic liminal play

i am a balm to the dead

i am the loose ends of the testimonial exhaust fumes of my life

    more of what was required
    or of what was never expected
    the i of witness and remains

i am

the subject

of

collective collaborative
deep-six surveillance
of the young who sit limber in their tweet
curled in their appeal

hoping
      the i's
          will
             slip
               still
          so one
          could say

that wannabe martyr

he "fell" lingually "hard"

less than icarus
more than circus performer
less than nuanced
more than testimonial
less than lyrical
more than prosaic
even almost never the bard
maybe minstrel

my punjabi nostrils curling out
ol factoring the present washed up on the past

like gang ah ma
viscous in the present
seeing ah
sideways

i am of
a sway way
moment   with no ambition

i am

        subject

to

cantankerous outbreaks of silence

claused in by careering possibilities

proffering candid conversation

conceptual acrobatics assault
the senses over a beer

those who memorialize their lives in pages set for them
the invitation to memory
cue taking
to distill the distillation of the mind

the obesity in idea

cellulite dimples drape off an unmovable tv tragedy
thick lined in each winged moment
pau-city of
nutrient value
weighted in anger
celluloid "other" dimple
draping over the unmovable tragedy

a gold standard worn with pride
the triple-cheeked, double-breasted, xtra-larged, enriched chair
unified static analogy
unwaivered direction toward definitive belief
this just path and the hurtle into catastrophe

spiralled charcoal night
as we descend again
watching the pinhole light
move upward away

i loved you first, i love you now
i will love you when neither of us are beside each other
but my beloved
this is the other torture session

extended credit line, lifeline, love line, laugh line, soup line, kitchen line
i want to buy an extra life, create an avatar, i want my humanity virtualized
i want my showcase line
the promised fifteen seconds
the hollywood red-carpet line in my living room
paparazzi flicks from the malfunctioning lights above the sink
i want my hair to be a line of pure curls

the line of acquisition
the line of acquiescence
the hard line that appears after concern and loss
the martial line that becomes commodity

the non-line between war and open investment
a placeholder line for a global everything

the line to the closest circle
the inner circle of circles
the dialogic obfuscation i want a line

                        that sets me free

singe me a line ... *tell me*
me stories

the in finite line of the capital
r.o.i. / ism lining my polypsed colon
the syndicate anonymous
solvent and recapitalized
launder the world
repackage yesterday
regift it today

      I do it for my children and my grandchildren
      I did it for you
      I did it for them
      I do it to save mankind
      I do it to save the idea of saving
      I want to give back
      I want to back the give
      I want a writeoff
      I want that tax deduction on the give
      I want to find the loop and hole it

      I did it to you
      I did it to them
      I make it happen to make an impact
      My line is in the belly of the beast
      I'll take 10 per cent of that
      Call me old school and
      I am confessing I am moving forward
      I will move you forward

repatriate this symbol
restore the archaeologized artifact
hot with denied ritual and life
after the retail nation and vale of usury
line it up for a capital repurchase
the full market value exhausted from profit taken
now returned to original owner
without investiture and reparation

a man steps

a man steps
onto the pv centro
he has lost already

talks and speaks american

thinks and emotes latino

his a.m. road began

at the building of salvation

a bible in one hand

a saviour to the lost

redemption

the sinner
the aggrieved
the broken
the damaged
the dead-eyed sadist who found heaven
while descending into hell

more than the lord's wine

the night did not nourish

as he staggered off the rail

how lingua and i met in conversation

lingers ... fragrance
lime on sleeve
licorice smile

lingers
pears small
in the crease
of the palm

peeling preambles
flickering words
pulsating amid a figured candle
shadows swaying from hand to waist
arching upward

incisor
crunching on
soft sunlit peach flesh
the cool dew
collecting in droplets from your lips

perhaps
the nautical mile
undulating rippling
breakout crescendo

> *will we always do this?*
> *the way we end sentences ... how you capture my lips*
> *in your conclusion*

the sun's sliver
rolled between our fingers
touching ... burning ... searing
incinerating desire on a bevy of lilacs

to fill
your alcove soul
with a candle
this finger's nib
a lover's inscription
scribed in a curved flame on your back

> *the world will know you are my beloved*
> *and I am the chasm of your muse*

the flicker
off the clear crystal shroud
draping from your bosom

lingers
lighting up your halo
my blue flame finger
running up each soft disk
nudge into the soft spaces
a paper-thin nail
creasing your skin within
stretched you disappear

into a droplet fallen from a cerulean sky

in the room

i am claudius writing epitaphs
this life a small interlude

i always engender a forgetting
with those i meet

the hushed sweet-honeyed amnesiac smoke curled
stretch my barren lips
the crowd cacophonous
ready in retreat
fear
the tail end
of a ragged thought
i never forget(s) the fallacy in small things
friends chuckling in the after breeze

a small clatter of guards
the horn sounds
eyes brow up in curved inquisition
this claudius ... this quasi-something
limps along this line
a spring spire shatters against blue steel
my echo this babbled confession
laughter sheets downward
dead leaves, twigs, mulched flowers, and stones

okay then – if you will and ask of it

> *father*
> *forgive me in parcels*
> *this word drenched forehead*
> *recludes into the shade*
> *my next path*
> *inshallah*
> *will be hope*

havana christmas – five interludes

i. – the city speaks

in the notes of a fringe city
satchmo's whisper
"when it's sleepy time down south"
cobble step
tall small rooms
miniature christmas trees
yesterday's trumpet
spoken today

once a shoe to leathered limb
once a keystroke to king and queen
once a song sung to revolt a locution

a birthday time for sweet natasha
your deep sleep breath breaks in vancouver
between the jam sessions at teatros of brittle havana
malecón spray prayers upward
amid crumbling fury

ii. – in the season

a poem wanders in heaven
on burning pavement
the heel of word will not nourish
the soul of small trees
from tall narrow houses
my babies
my present
my spinal green
a voice anchor wails
horsehair string on atomic vibration
the extended note
strait crackle spray
mute the music in my mind

… 'tis the season
… 'tis a season
havana has no snow
jack frost finds it too hot down here
frosty and the reindeers are grainy
watched by those who are watched
bundled together in tight corner rooms

satchmo a lonely trumpet
prado to el capitolio
a wraith silhouette
voice vibrates
i cough a gravel prayer where he stood
lonely trumpet

a piano hand thumps against a charcoal night
elusive perfect note
that is not on the sheet

to play this music
who is this solitary player translucent in light
who is this cuban trumpet

iii. – the hurricane music

swirl a sound
this hurricane music
the sax talks to piano
charcoal sky showers him with blessings
an angel in a luminous jacket
ill-cropped pants

bass words
with drums

a swirl … a swirl

hip swivel

quick two-step forward

one step back

one pant leg

caressed by two warm muscular thighs

iv. – we and i

wet rattle frenzy
bones before ghost
of bones
our bodies
in music there is life
or as satch' said
"we don't play music, we play life"
season a liner note
verse a conversation
sight a canvas
baroque skin on porcelain
mauve bleeds in red
eye a deep chocolate
skin curve

this city

this play

this hurried cane

out

v. – homecoming

i'm coming home
learning to smile
my zigzag life line
field to field
work to word to work
family
i'm in the season
with jack frosty and the reindeers
and they're all learning new tunes
i'm back to big presents in medium-sized homes
in the moment
coming home to you   V
hearing old satch'
and something of the world
    looking straight up with those sad eyes
    living with those broken promises

i'm coming home
to a place called *wonderful*

where love resides

(for jane)

slow curve of the midriff
eyes creasing up in smile
eyes searching the sands, the sadness
regret exhaled
into the full wind of the tide
on a fall evening

brimful of laughter
we laugh at the smallness of the world
sharing the laugh, watch it subside
as it dissipates out to the sea
quietly we love   and part
watching the waves slap against the rocks

this turn of self again
hands remain against the border of our hurts
each finger yearns for tendrils to reconnect
the heaviness of a hand
emotional concrete
the unwavering past
and yet, even then
the warmth returns

neural synapses converge
release, course
through the mesh of consciousness
a symphony, empathy restores itself
concrete hearts gather sunflowers radiating outward
up through arteries, those veined fibres pulse out
move our fingers together
and we arrive

where we started

ACKNOWLEDGEMENTS

dream / arteries developed over many years and has been informed by the generosity and kindness of friends, researchers, and writers.

I would like to thank everyone at Talonbooks for their commitment to the writer and the books produced – Kevin Williams, Vicki Williams, Greg Gibson, Ann-Marie Metten, Les Smith, Chloë Filson, and Spencer Williams.

I also want to thank my friend and this collection's final editor, Jeff Derksen, for his careful and well-considered editorial suggestions as we worked to meet deadline.

I am grateful to the Banff Centre Literary Arts Programs and former program director Steven Ross Smith and his staff for including my work, my interests, and my ideas; I also want to thank the Banff Centre 2014 In(ter)ventions residency and in particular faculty resident Roy Miki. Roy, a friend, teacher, and mentor, worked with me through the manuscript and specifically the final stages of the *Komagata Maru* suite of poems; also gratitude to In(ter)ventions faculty member Carla Harryman, who also provided further thoughts on the *Komataga Maru* poem series while I was in residence. To my co-interveners – a cohort of fine scribes – I say thank you. I also want to extend my sincere appreciation to Fred Wah, who first encouraged me to consider the residency and has quietly supported my mind's work for many years.

Much gratitude to the *Komagata Maru 100 Centenary Anniversary Project – Generations, Geographies, and Echoes* and to the community partners who worked so diligently to make it happen and who included my work in the programming. The centenary project was a major event initiative that was expertly managed by project manager and community historian and curator Naveen Girn. Thank you.

To friends who had a part in encouraging my writing, some of who read earlier versions of this book – Wayde Compton, Taryn Hubbard, Larissa Lai, Carmen Papalia, Jason Sunder, and Jordan Strom; to Michael Turner for good friendship and advice in placing the book; and to my friend Ashok Mathur for his support over the years.

To my long-time friend and mentor Sadhu Binning for teaching me about the *Komagata Maru* history so many years ago and for many years of generosity, I thank you for this knowledge and the books you shared with me, including the obscure scholarly works about the Ghadar Party that told so much more of the story.

To my family, Jane Cleary Dulai, Natasha Seta Cleary Dulai, and Nadya Gita Cleary Dulai. Thank you for your love, your presence, and your validation.

Previously published

Some poems in this collection previously appeared in the following online and print publications or were read on the following radio and television programs:

- An earlier version of "letter to the *maru*" was published in the anti-racism issue of *Rungh* 4 (1998): 43–46.

- "dereliction suite" was previously published in the Roy Miki special issue of *West Coast Line: Contemporary Writing and Criticism* 42.1 (Spring 2008): 142–44.

- Earlier versions of "*chita* – 100 lines to die," "*rakhri*," and "asiancy: a word" were published in *Open Text: Canadian Poetry and Poetics in the 21st Century*, vol. 2. Roger Farr, ed. Vancouver: Cue Books, 2009. 38–43.

- An earlier version of "asiancy: a word" was also published in *Tracing the Lines: Reflections on Contemporary Poetics and Cultural Politics in Honour of Roy Miki*. Maia Joseph, Christine Kim, Larissa Lai, and Christopher Lee, eds. Vancouver: Talonbooks, 2012. 86.

- "presence" was posted June 7, 2012, to the Writing section of *Offerings*, an online collaborative and multidisciplinary arts-based platform created by Canadian Metis artist France Trépanier to explore indigenous and other cultural forms of offerings.

- "mourning ghazals" was previously published in *The Capilano Review* 2.49 (Spring 2006): 98.

- "ash" was published in *Canadian Literature* 208 (Spring 2011): 108.

- Earlier versions of "smile," the epigraph on page 30, and "atomic eeyore" were previously published in the Heirlooms edition of *Memewar* 5 (2008): 39–41.

- "dereliction suite," "how lingua and i met in conversation," and "smile" were read on the CBC Television national variety program *ZeD TV* in November 2004.

- "havana christmas – five interludes" was commissioned for CBC Radio One's national radio program *Sounds Like Canada*, Winter 2001.

- "*it-dhé* (here), a vancouver special circa 1980" was first published in the Vancouver 125 edition of *subTerrain* 59 (2011): 26.

- "after tomorrow" first appeared in *Matrix* 63 (Spring 2003).

dream / arteries relies on numerous sources that helped shape the "soul-journ to the end of the pacific" section of the book, which includes the "epistle to the reader (confidential)," the "letter to the *maru*," and a suite of poems.

The "epistle to the reader" serves as a counterpoint to the archival record and is formatted to evoke a letter dated June 8, 1914, from Inspector Malcolm Reid (Dominion Immigration Agent) to Superintendent of Immigration W.D. Scott – subject matter: starvation on the ship; surveillance of ship, Vancouver Archives, box 509-D-7, folder 2, reference code AM69, page 149. Quotations attributed to Inspector Reid are from the same source. The ship's registry listing that accompanies the introduction is compiled from information set out on the *Clyde Ships*, *Norway-Heritage*, and *The Ships List* websites.

When researching "letter to the *maru*," I drew on a number of sources to build a narrative that I hope the reader will find to be an immediate, visceral, and almost tactile experience. The idea was also to situate the issue squarely within the context of the plight of the Punjabi migrant (so I named the passenger Ranjeet). As time moved forward, Ranjeet became simply the "unknown passenger," given the very real legacies available both publicly and through the archival websites established since 1998, when an earlier form of the letter was first published.

One such archival site, the *Komagata Maru Journey* website, is a rich archival repository of primary government documents, newspaper clippings, historical photographs, videos, and interviews. The site includes two private collections donated to SFU Special Collections: the Indo-Canadian Oral History Collection (Dr. Hari Sharma) and the Kohaly Collection (Inderjit Singh Kohaly). I would like to thank SFU liaison librarian Moninder Bubber for assisting me with this website and for answering the many queries I have posed over the past two years.

Additional sources for "letter to the *maru*" include:

- Johnston, Hugh J.M. *The Voyage of the Komagata Maru: The Sikh Challenge to Canada's Colour Bar*. Vancouver: UBC Press, 1989, expanded and fully revised 2014.

- Ferguson, Ted. *A White Man's Country: An Exercise in Canadian Prejudice*. Toronto: Doubleday Canada, 1975.

- Puri, Harish K. *Ghadar Movement to Bhagat Singh: A Collection of Essays*. Chandigarh, India: Unistar, 2012.

- Miranda, F., and G. Flores Méndez. "Mass Arrival: De-Colonial Aesthetics in Action." Available on the University of Oxford Centre for Criminology *Border Criminologies* website, 2013.

- Darling, Sir Malcolm. *The Punjab Peasant in Prosperity and Debt*. London: Oxford UP, 1947.

- Singh, Gurpreet. *Why Mewa Singh Killed William Hopkinson? Revisiting the Murder of a Canadian Immigration Inspector*. Surrey, B.C.: Chetna, 2013.

Sources for the British colonial structures imposed on the farming communities in Punjab include the following:

- Rai, Lala Lajpat. *Young India: An Interpretation and a History of the Nationalist Movement from Within*. New York: Huebsch, 1916; republished HindustanBooks.com, 2012.

- Hyndman, Henry Mayers. "Reports of the Social Democratic Federation, Ruin of India by British Rule." *Histoire de la IIe Internationale* 16 (1907), Geneva: Minkoff Reprint, 1978. 513–33.

- Sunderland, Jabez T. *The Causes of Famine in India*. [Toronto] [1905, printed from transactions of the Canadian Institute, December 3, 1904]; reprinted Ann Arbor, MI: HathiTrust Digital Library, 2010.

- *Wikipedia* sources, including "A Few Facts about British Rule in India."

A number of references to India's financial tributes and taxation regimes under the British Raj have been cited as primary reasons for the level of human suffering that took place during this time. The references I used were from the following:

- The work of journalist, author, and equality advocate William Digby (active 1878–1901), including *"Prosperous" British India: A Revelation from Official Records*. London: Unwin, 1901.

- Swami Abhedananda (Kaliprasad Chandra). *India and Her People*. Satish Chandra Mukherjee, ed. New York: Vedanta Society, 1906.

- Adams, Brooks. *The Law of Civilization and Decay: An Essay on History*. London: MacMillan, 1895.

Quotations from Vancouver residents and editorial comments at the time are from the Vancouver *Sun* and *Province* archives, including "Boat Load of Hindus on the Way to Vancouver" (Vancouver *Sun*, June 19, 1914) and various other articles published in April and May 1914. Thanks to Shannon Miller for confirming some of the information related to reportage of the *Komagata Maru* in this newspaper.

In "soul-journ to the end of the pacific," the quotation from Gurdit Singh that opens the section is from an article published in the *Daily News Advertiser* on May 23, 1914.

In "letter to the *maru*," the quotation that begins "We extend a cordial welcome to Bhai Gurdit Singh ..." is from articles published in *The Hindustanee* on June 1, 1914, and in the Vancouver *Sun* on June 19, 1914.

In "letter to the *maru*," the quotation from Dr. Oscar Douglas Skelton is from O.D. Skelton, *Life and Letters of Sir Wilfrid Laurier*, vol. 2. Toronto: S.B. Gundy, Oxford UP, 1921. 352n1.

In "diese störrisch haken," the epigraph is taken from the *Norway-Heritage* website.

In "my name is *sicilia*, you called me saviour once," the epigraph is an imagined, pseudo-archival record.

In "the redness of things," the quote by J.E. Bird is from page 2 of meeting minutes held in the City of Vancouver Archives, box 509-D-7, folder 2, reference code AM69 – H.H Stevens, page 239 (available on the *Komagata Maru Journey* website).

In "subedhar, sub alt din, alter-sub-alt-in," the epigraph is from a letter by Prime Minister Robert Borden to Hon. G.H. Perley, High Commissioner to Great Britain, dated July 17, 1914 (available on the *Komagata Maru Journey* website).

In "(psalms) to the four clergy," the epigraphs from the court testimony of Mewa Singh are from proceedings of trial titled "In the court of Oyer & Terminer & General Gaol Delivery." Vancouver Fall Assizes. (Before The Honorable Mr. Justice Morrison.) Vancouver, B.C. October 30, 1914. Rex v. Mewa Singh. (Murder.) A.D. Taylor, Esq., K.C. for the Crown. E.M.N. Woods, Esq., for the Accused, page 26 (available on the *Komagata Maru Journey* website).

In "to settle the prairies," the epigraph is from a web page titled "Clifford Sifton and Canada's Immigration Policy" on the *British Immigrants in Montreal* website written by Deborah Waddell-Robertson, 2009–2014. The Clifford Sifton quote was published in Sir Clifford Sifton, "The Immigrants Canada Wants," *Maclean's*, April 1, 1922: 16, 32–34.

Definitions for the Japanese words comprising "*Komagata Maru*" are from the following sources:

- "Japanese Pronouns," *Wikipedia*
- "Japanese Ship-Naming Conventions," *Wikipedia*
- "Koma" + "Kata" on *EUdict.com*
- "City of Vancouver Archives" on the *City of Vancouver* website

The archival photographs that accompany the text in the "soul-journ to the end of the pacific" section are described more fully in a section following these notes. In particular, the photograph on page 34 shows a Sikh passenger who wears an elaborate head ornament or insignia that reminded me of the Nihang Sikhs; this is a rare image onboard a ship where many of the passengers were British Indian Army veterans. As the photo is not sourced to what day it was taken, it is not clear why the Sikh would decide to adorn his turban with this ceremonial symbol. Nihang Sikhs were for centuries at the forefront of the battles when Sikh armies battled the Mughals, neighbouring Hindu rulers, and of course the British.

In "from sea to sun," the epigraph is from a Canadian Council for Refugees FOI–obtained document "Marine Migrants: Program Strategy for the Next Arrival," September 2013. Now posted on the *Canadian Council for Refugees* website.

In "wisconsin temple poems: temple the prayer," the italicized stanzas are adapted from verses in the early section of the Guru Granth Sahib as published on the *Raj Karega Khalsa* website, although the last stanza reframes Psalm 23 from the Bible, particularly the notion of the Lord protecting those who are passing into death.

In "investigative erasure," the redacted passages are from a November 20, 2012, press release issued by the Milwaukee Division of the Federal Bureau of Investigation with the title "Oak Creek Sikh Temple Shooting Investigation Conclusion."

The title "in the room" is inspired by a line in "The Love Song of J. Alfred Prufrock" by T.S. Eliot.

In "re-word," the "*I'm so sin-surr*" line is a riff by Cedric the Entertainer in Jay-Z's song "threat" on *the black album*, 2003.

The archival photos illustrating "soul-journ to the end of the pacific" appear courtesy of the following sources:

insert 1   SS *Stubbenhuk*. Deutsches Schiffahrtsmuseum, Bremerhaven.

page xi   SS *Stubbenhuk*. Deutsches Schiffahrtsmuseum, Bremerhaven.

insert 2   "Sikh men and boy onboard the Komagata Maru," ca. May 23–July 23, 1914. Gurdit Singh wearing light-coloured suit, white beard, left foreground. Leonard Frank photo. Vancouver Public Library Special Collections 6231.

page 11   Detail from "Sikhs aboard ship, Komagata Maru," 1914. Canadian Photo Company photo. Vancouver Public Library Special Collections 136.

page 12   "Indian immigrants on board the Komogata Maru [*sic*] in English Bay, Vancouver, British Columbia," 1914. [John] Woodruff Album photo. LAC PA-034015.

page 14   Detail from "Sikhs on board the 'Komogata [*sic*] Maru' in English Bay, Vancouver, British Columbia," 1914. [John] Woodruff Album photo. LAC PA-034014.

page 16   "Mewa Singh funeral procession 1915," January 11, 1915. Photographer unknown. *Komagata Maru Journey* website. Node 15151.

page 17   "Mewa Singh funeral pyre," January 11, 1915. Photographer unknown. Plate from Norman Buchignani, Doreen M. Indra, and Ram Srivastava. *Continuous Journey: A Social History of South Asians in Canada*. Toronto: McClelland and Stewart, 1985. *Komagata Maru Journey* website. Node 3463.

page 20   Detail from "Sikhs on board the 'Komogata [*sic*] Maru' in English Bay, Vancouver, British Columbia," 1914. [John] Woodruff Album photo. LAC PA-034014.

page 31   "Komagata Maru at sea," 1914. Stuart Thomson photo. Vancouver Public Library Special Collections 6225.

page 32   "The Komagata Maru and the HMCS Rainbow in Vancouver Harbour," ca. May 23–July 23, 1914. Leonard Frank photo. Vancouver Public Library Special Collections 6229.

page 33   "Sikh men and boy onboard the Komagata Maru," ca. May 23–July 23, 1914. Gurdit Singh wearing light-coloured suit, white beard, left foreground. Leonard Frank photo. Vancouver Public Library Special Collections 6231.

page 34   Detail from "Komagata Maru incident," 1914. Canadian Photo Company photo. Vancouver Public Library Special Collections 133.

page 35   Copy of letter dated June 8, 1914, for Inspector Malcolm Reid (Dominion Immigration Agent) to Superintendent of Immigration W.D. Scott – subject matter: starvation on the ship; surveillance of ship. City of Vancouver Archives, box 509-D-7, folder 2, reference code AM69, page 149. Also available on the *Komagata Maru Journey* website.

page 36-t   "Spectators in small boats in the Vancouver harbour during the Komagata Maru incident," ca. May 23–July 23, 1914. Canadian Photo Company. Vancouver Public Library Special Collections 124.

page 36-b   "Malcolm Reid, H.H. Steven during Komagata Maru incident," 1914. Photographer unknown. Vancouver Public Library Special Collections 6228.

page 37   Detail from "Sikh people on board the Komagata Maru," 1914. Canadian Photo Company. Vancouver Public Library Special Collections 121.

page 38   Detail from "Sikhs aboard ship, Komagata Maru," 1914.
               Canadian Photo Company photo. Vancouver Public
               Library Special Collections 136.

page 39   Detail from "Komagata Maru incident," 1914. Canadian Photo
               Company. Vancouver Public Library Special Collections 122.

page 40   "The Komagata Maru and the HMCS Rainbow," ca. May 23–
               July 23, 1914. Canadian Photo Company. Vancouver Public
               Library Special Collections 134.

insert 3   Detail from "Komagata Maru leaving Vancouver,"
               July 23, 1914. Leonard Frank photo. Vancouver Public Library
               Special Collections 16639.

Phinder Dulai is the Vancouver-based author of two previous books of poetry: *Ragas from the Periphery* (Arsenal Pulp Press, 1995) and *Basmati Brown* (Nightwood Editions, 2000). His most recent work has been published in *Canadian Literature* and *Open Text: Canadian Poetry and Poetics in the 21st Century*, vol. 3 (Cue Books, 2013). Earlier work appeared in *Ankur*, *Canadian Ethnic Studies*, *Capilano Review*, *Matrix*, *Memewar*, *Rungh*, *subTerrain*, *Toronto South Asian Review*, and *West Coast Line*. Dulai is a co-founder of the Surrey-based interdisciplinary contemporary arts group the South of Fraser Inter-Arts Collective (SOFIA/C).